P9-DOB-958

450

THE ROLLING STONE BOOK OF
COMEDY

THE ROLLING STONE BOOK OF
COMEDY

Photographs by Bonnie Schiffman
Text by Bill Zehme
Introduction by Billy Crystal

A BULFINCH PRESS BOOK
LITTLE, BROWN AND COMPANY
BOSTON   TORONTO   LONDON

For Esther, Nancy and Grace
— B.S.
For Lucy
— B.Z.

PHOTO EDITOR: LAURIE KRATOCHVIL
DESIGNER: NANCY BUTKUS
PRODUCED BY SARAH LAZIN BOOKS

Copyright © 1991 by Sarah Lazin Books
Photographs copyright ©1991 by Bonnie Schiffman
Text copyright ©1991 by Bill Zehme
Introduction copyright ©1991 by Billy Crystal

All rights reserved. No part of this book may be reproduced in any form
or by any electronic or mechanical means, including information storage
and retrieval systems, without permission in writing from the publisher,
except by a reviewer who may quote brief passages in a review.

First Edition

ISBN 0-8212-1848-4
Library of Congress Catalog Number 91-55468
Library of Congress Cataloging-in-Publication information is available.

Bulfinch Press is an imprint and trademark of
Little, Brown and Company (Inc.)
Published simultaneously in Canada by
Little, Brown & Company (Canada) Limited

PRINTED IN THE UNITED STATES OF AMERICA

PREFACE

There has never been a funny sentence written about comedy. Comedy is like that. One cannot improve upon the purity of its premise. We can poke it with sticks, turn it over in the light, take blood and urine samples, but we will never make complete sense of it. Laughter is an involuntary act, up there with the sneeze in its utter peculiarity. We laugh to keep from weeping or, worse, running through the streets with firearms and power tools. Comedy, then, is reflexive, an antidote to unspeakable ills, somehow spoken anyway. (Correctly executed, it does not soothe, but either distracts us or reorders our angst.) In the lifetime of ROLLING STONE, which comprises a quarter century of cultural witness-bearing, comedy saved America. Faced with unpleasant alternatives, we as a nation learned to Make Fun Of that which we could not understand — as well as that which we understood perfectly well, but did not especially like. Much fun was made, necessarily so. Bad times, they say, bring good comedy. Industrious men and women saw this period as one rife with great career opportunity. So they went forth and leavened. Those who excelled were proclaimed heroes. They exchanged the fruit of their inner turmoil for big, boffo laughs, thereby fortifying us so that we could go on with our small and desperate lives. This book stands as an homage to these same practitioners, who gave of themselves so freely and, in return, gained only enormous wealth, fame and power. The faces collected between these covers represent a vast cross section of Comedy People from various media, old school and new school alike. (Remember: There would be no new school if there had been no old school from which to steal.) As such, this volume does not aspire to be encyclopedic; it is, instead, a spectrum of comic styles that shaped a generation's sense of humor. It is about evoking comic spirit, through words and through pictures worth tens of thousands of words. It is about being funny in an era when being funny mattered more than ever.

— B.Z.

INTRODUCTION

Posing for pictures is my least favorite thing in the world. I don't look forward to it. I can't wait for it to be over. The whole process is painful for me. If people see you as a funny person, they immediately think that's the side of you the camera has to capture. "You're a funny guy," photographers always tell me, "so just get silly, be spontaneous, make some faces. . . ." *Disaster*. It's unbelievably difficult to make the same face thirty-six times in a row. I always end up looking like one of the flying monkeys from *The Wizard of Oz*.

Photographers sometimes forget that I want to feel good when I look at the picture. I don't want to look like an extra from *8 1/2* , some renegade from a Fellini movie. It's very important to me that I be captured the right way, because that's the way my fans get to meet me. They can hold the picture up two inches from their faces and talk to me if they want.

Bonnie Schiffman understands that. She also realizes that there's more to a funny person than just being funny. She knows something inside is making him be funny, and that's the part of him she tries to capture. My pictures with Bonnie are rarely funny shots. And when we try to be funny, they're not as good as the moodier shots that I think show the real me.

What draws me out is that Bonnie has this great personality — she has a great soul. Our sessions aren't, "Give me more, baby, baby, give me more, pout for me, pout for me!" She knows if I don't want to do something, there's no way she's going to reach me, so she leaves me be. She also has a wonderful sense of humor. When somebody laughs at the right things, you know you're okay: Bonnie laughs at the right things. If I can make her laugh, I feel good, and if she can make me laugh, I feel better.

An inventive person, Bonnie won't let me put my hand near my face unless I'm holding something, like a rattle. Every time I put my hand on my cheek, she'll say, "1977." You know those early composite shots, hand on the face, little smile: "Oh, I'm a funny guy!" (Most comics and actors, by the way, have to have their hands surgically removed from their faces.)

Bonnie is a good motivator in that she makes you stretch to come up with something different. She poses you in a manner that makes you *uncomfortable* a little bit, by putting an obstacle in your way, some odd-shaped little thing. When Bonnie starts a session with, "You know what I was thinking . . . ?" right away you know it's going to be an adventure. She'll have a chair that looks like Picasso threw up on it. It's on a weird angle so you can't sit quite right or your leg has to go someplace else — some little twist that makes you work. You don't think you're working, but you end up working.

For instance, we had this duck. It was for a magazine shoot, and I went to Bonnie's house, where she works, and she told me I'd be opening presents for this Christmas issue and I'd be wearing pajamas. I went, "Weeellll maybe, let me see, I don't know about the pajamas." Because I worry about the Goon Factor. When I hit the Goon Factor, *bzzzzzzzzzzz*, the buzzers go off and I think the comedy police are going to come and take me away. She said, "Open this box," and when I did, there was a live duck in there, wearing a bow tie made out of the same material as my pajamas. I spent the whole day with this little duck either sitting on my head or making on my lap, while there was this pained expression on my face. Still, as duck shots go, it was a *really good* duck shot.

Bonnie understands funny people. A perfect example: Robin Williams is the most exciting comic performer working today. Bonnie's

photos of Robin are electric, because that's who he is — he's a comet. There's a really wonderful photo of Whoopi Goldberg, which is more of a sexy shot than a funny shot. Marty Short is an eccentric wild man who's a great effervescent soul. That will be in his photos. Her concept for each person is not so much about what comedy is, but about who the person is that she's photographing — and that's a big difference.

Being photographed is much more intimate than people realize. In some ways, it's harder than playing a part, because you have to be yourself, and you know that it's being captured instantly and millions of people are going to see this picture. You have to unfold to the lens and to the photographer and trust that she's going to capture who you want people to see.

Bonnie has a hallway in her house with all of her favorite shots on it. I'd done several sessions with her, and I had never been on the wall. So every time I went in there, I'd hit her with, "I guess my picture's not good enough to be on the wall."

I finally made the wall — but not with a funny picture. It's a sunset shot, all in silhouette, of me holding my horse that I love. When I see this photo, I think, Yeah, *that's me*. She captured my whole experience, my whole relationship with this horse. Let me make a baseball analogy: Mickey Mantle once told me, "I hit 536 home runs, but there were only 20 when I felt I really got all of it."

In this one picture, in just a split second, Bonnie got all of it. She caught a side of myself that is more revealing of me than any other portraits I have. It's a beauty, a fabulous photo. When I look at this shot, I understand why I actually enjoy being before Bonnie's camera.

BILLY CRYSTAL
LOS ANGELES, 1991

Chevy Chase and Dan Aykroyd

The camera never laughs; people do. Once, long ago, they knew instant crowd approval, instant guffaw; they heard laughs while they performed. Now that they are movie boys, there must be silence — *quiet on the set* — when they deserve response. It's too damned quiet, anymore.

They fled New York, the live broadcasts of Saturday nights, the weekly sketch-drugs-and-rock-and-roll revue, the LIVENESS! They fled, alas, for movie careers. And yet if they'd done nothing other than television, they would have already done enough. Once they worked fast; now they work slow, for better pay. (Interesting how the quick stuff is more difficult to forget: We know that the Landshark made housecalls, but did *Doctor Detroit*?) Still, they cannot break old habits: Danny continues to work on perfecting new impersonations never to be seen beyond his bathroom mirror. "Just for my own entertainment," he says. Chevy finds himself raking headlines for Weekend Update material more than a decade after abdicating his anchor post. Back then, Emily Litella called him Cheddar Cheese. The truth is, he is still Cheddar Cheese, and you're still not.

Tracey Ullman

Clearly, she is never alone. Voices live in her head. "They've said my brain is like a spinning radio dial." Listen. "I do voices all the time." She will steal your soul and play it back for you while you wait. "I don't think there are any that I can't do if I listen long enough." She is siphoning you now, even if you think otherwise. "There's no accent that I can't do." She is British espionage, a life spy, an undercover sponge. When dimpling the seat cushions of talk shows, she is something of a candied nerve-ending, a peppermint synapse. That is diversion. That is her ruse. At core, she is sifting for dark secrets. Everywhere, she sees sadness and truth. "Even when I was five, a clown would come up to me and say, 'Hullo, I'm Captain Billy's Banana!' And I'd go, *'Don't be so bloody stupid! Don't patronize me! I'm six next week!'"*

Gilbert Gottfried

His eyes are shut. He can't see anything. He can't see. He can't see. His eyes are shut. They're shut. They are beyond shut. They are not open. He can't open his eyes. They never open. For God's sake, his eyes are closed! Is there no decency? Can we not afford him decency? Where is the decency? Not in his eyes. Here is what is in his eyes: nothing! There's nothing in his eyes. His eyes are shut! What could get in his eyes? Nothing. Try putting something in your eyes if your eyes are shut. Go ahead. We can wait. We're waiting. Nothing, right? That's because you shut your eyes. Your eyes are shut. They're shut. They could have been open. But now they are shut.

George Burns and Bob Hope

Together they are older than many rock formations. If they calcified, they would be monuments. They are partners in survival, having survived even their partners. George had Gracie; Hope had Crosby. Now they have vaudeville memories and California real estate. Burns is the straight man, who lived to bend. Hope is all hook, as hooked as his grand sloping proboscis or a slice into the rough at Pebble Beach. They cannot be stopped, for which we must at least marvel and at most envy. Call it drive. To wit, around Hollywood, one can motor onto either Bob Hope Drive or George Burns Road (which dead-ends into Cedars-Sinai Hospital — fine irony, Burns must have thought).

In some ways, they are all they have left. But consider this: Hope has a prized possession, which hangs in the den of his Toluca Lake compound: a photograph of General George Patton pissing into the Rhine. Metaphorically, both of the aged jesters here have done the same thing. "I've been offered a lot of damned money for that," Hope has said of the picture. "But I'm never gonna give it up."

Judy Tenuta

Can a truly feminine woman stand alone with microphone and demand attention? Can a woman be blithe and ephemeral and utter provocative observations, gauged to bestir ovation? Will men not be intimidated by such attempts, laugh uneasily, and privately seek harbor in the company of those who are less challenging? Does the one who calls herself the Petite Flower concern herself with such existential trifles? Hardly. Birds live in her tresses, so delicate is she. Behind her squeeze box, she demurely suggests to followers, "Worship me, pigs!" And they do, for they must. "It's reality," she has said. "Eat it."

As her mother would say, "You have to forgive her."

Jeff Altman

He has been known to feign unconsciousness in crowded restaurants. He collapses to the floor and refuses to get up. For this reason, Letterman greatly enjoys the pleasure of his company. "He makes me laugh harder, just kind of goofing around in the afternoon, than any other comedian I've ever spent any time with," says Dave, who is, as we know, a discerning man. "He's best when he's just performing in the community at large." Long ago, Altman performed on television as the Jeff in *Pink Lady and Jeff*, perhaps the worst show in the medium's history, on which he worked with two confused Japanese pop stars. His survival is what is so exemplary. He stands resurrected, a man who likes his butt steak and isn't afraid to admit it in clubs throughout the land. "Mmmm, sweet and meaty," he says, and people cannot help but cheer.

David Steinberg

Sometimes he would dine with Groucho, a young charge at the elbow of a master, and just how much the master charged is anyone's guess. Steinberg has long been the great charmer of comedy, in whose hands we feel relaxed and well-considered. He is the comedian who, more than any other, seems most likely to smell good. "He's a professional pussycat," wrote Albert Goldman, disapprovingly, but he was probably just jealous. Because Steinberg is a sweet-faced fellow, his bite always comes without warning, except that it always comes. He owned Watergate, for instance. He likened Nixon's face to a bare foot sorely in need of a sock. The FBI kept a file on him. "Booga booga," he said, and so, too, did America. On *The Smothers Brothers Comedy Hour*, he mocked Moses, because of which the Smothers Brothers lost their comedy hour. Whereupon, the network gave *him* a show. "Nothing is as fleeting," he has said, "as a moment of wit on television."

Julie Brown

Where goeth The Comedienne? To the Hot Dog Stand in Inappropriate Clothing? Well, yes. But where, in a Larger Sense, goeth The Comedienne? She is not a stand-up nor is she exactly a funny actress; rather, The Comedienne is a fully-formed *persona*. Lucy, for instance. Lucy, for eternity. But Lucy is gone. And, lately, most women are uncomfortable with that belabored French spelling: *comedienne*. It sounds fussy and prim, but it is a fine old word, really. The problem now is that there are too few who wish to inhabit it and fewer still, present company excepted, who are able to inhabit it with requisite pluck and verve and lovely, unbridled foolishness.

Carl Reiner

He is the picture of restraint. He prides himself on his ability not to break up. On *Your Show of Shows*, working live with Caesar, he never laughed. "We *never* laughed on camera," he has said significantly. (Sketch comedy lives and dies by the straight face.) Reiner was the first great Second Banana of Television, Caesar's principle support beam. Ever since, he has withheld himself, so that others could go forth and be embraced. In this way, he became a comic Midas: He created Rob and Laura Petrie, now and forever the J.F.K. and Jackie of sitcomdom. (He played Alan Brady, a despot with and without hair.) It was Reiner who was sober inquisitor to Mel Brooks's Two-Thousand-Year-Old Man. Later, he directed God in a movie, which also featured George Burns. Also, he brought Steve Martin to film and kept bringing him back until both got it right. Still, of all that he has done, he will always be proud of what he did not do. "I didn't laugh," he said. "I held myself together."

Keenen Ivory Wayans and Kim Wayans

They are two of nine sibling Wayans, who found closeness and comedy (a great link) in a Manhattan housing project. "When we walked to school, the older ones held the younger ones' hands," said Keenen, the second-oldest, and so he does still, when she will allow it. (She is one of several sibling Wayans who has worked under Keenen's aegis.) He has removed sanctimony from black (as in black man's) comedy and teased his own, as Jews tease their own, and WASPs, and Italians, and so on. Because he has done this in American living rooms — in living color, natch — he stands at the new forefront of television troublemakers, especially those who employ their relatives. "Next time anybody calls you nigger," his mother told him when he was a boy, "you tell them to call you Mr. Nigger." Respect has followed him ever since. And, of course, laughter.

Tom Hanks

He is certainly no wisenheimer, this Hanks. And, by this, we mean The Real Hanks. We expect arrogance, smugness, glibness. We expect rapier retorts and high-voltage banter. Instead he is courteous and sincere. His liquid eyes, with their almost Asian set, are even a bit melancholy. They are never quite mirthful. Yes, he is funny, but almost never frenetically so. His laugh is an old guy's laugh, a slow, lumbering, fogyish sort of *huh-huh-huh*. Yet he bursts with childlike enthusiasm, the font of his appeal, ultimately. The wonder of Hanks: He drives a Dodge Caravan, he says, because "I like sitting up high; it's nice to see what's causing the traffic jam." Whenever he spies an accident on the road, he lurches with excitement: *"Whoa! What happened here?"* When he stumbles upon a good parking spot, he crows: "Look at this! *Beeyooteeful!"* Even weather sparks him: "This rain is *crackin' me up!"*

Gary Larson

The people who name insects named one for this fellow: *Strigiphilus garylarsoni*. "The biting louse," he explained. "I didn't figure they'd give me a swan." Larson dwells in the furthermost reaches of questionable taste — *The Far Side*, if you will — where he comports himself like that rarest of specimens, The Fun Science Teacher. "I never sat down and said, You know, what the world needs is a good sick cartoonist," he has remarked, humbly. He is, of course, our *premier* sick cartoonist, whose mutant world is peopled with animals who behave like people and people who behave like animals. It is a bleak, unforgiving place, where, among other horrors, sharks eat children as a matter of course and somehow we are supposed to laugh and somehow we do. (Well, many of us do.) His own father once asked, "How come in your cartoons someone's always gonna get it?"

Roz Chast

Once, while driving across much of the nation on Interstate-80, she turned to her husband, who was behind the wheel, and asked, "What is the difference between concrete and cement?" Soon thereafter — for no answer would suffice — she assured him that if a big, mean guy ever beat him up in front of her, she'd probably not only scream for help, but also hit the big, mean guy with a vase. Such is the antic mind of one who commits great esoteric cartoonery, all gathered in book form. That which comprises subject matter in the Chast *oeuvre*, as described by the creator: "Odd occurrences; both well and poorly adjusted house pets; foods which have gone past their expiration dates; doilies; UFO's; old family recipes involving large cans of sweet potatoes; children who are overtired; sea salt; thread; and people you don't really know all that well."

Arsenio Hall

Comedy needs a man who can wear a hat. He has lots of hats.

"Arsenio offstage is the funniest person I've ever met in my life. He's the only person who can make me laugh until it gets dangerous, where you're going, 'Stop or else I'm gonna pee on myself!' He'll make me laugh until, like, two or three drops of pee come out. He just has the fastest mind and a knack for recalling obscurities — weird names from the past that make you giggle. For Arsenio, people like Jay Leno were his heroes. I think Jay Leno is talented, but I don't think he can fuck with Arsenio."

EDDIE MURPHY

"The dogs bark, but the caravan moves on."

ARAB PROVERB

John Goodman

O, to be a Big Lug! O, to be a Palooka! There is an art to being large the way Goodman is large. He looms genially. He comes untucked and rumpled and will belch the belch of kings. Also, he dances beautifully. It is essential in comic dealings for there to be a Big Guy. Sweet Big Guys are best, since they are easier to make fun of, without real threat of physical harm. Their gut absorbs the taunts; their smiles issue the warnings. Legend of the Big Guy: They say he once killed a man with his bear grin.

Spinal Tap

"Though neither a critics' nor a public favorite, Spinal Tap continues to fill a much needed void," read their listing in *Rocklopedia Brittanicus*, which of course does not actually exist, but then neither does Spinal Tap. Three men crawled inside the Beast that is satire and then they became the Beast. Rob Reiner directed them to do so in a mock rockumentary whose ramifications have been everlasting. There was Christopher Guest, who first saw stupefaction in metal heads, and told his friends; he became Nigel Tufnel, far right. Michael McKean became David St. Hubbins, far left. And masterparodist Harry Shearer was Derek Smalls. Together, they played subtly at playing louder than hell. They were so artfully bad they were forced to tour America in character, a living joke taken seriously. Groupies bared their breasts for them. "The closer we dared to get to the real thing," Shearer said, "the closer the real thing dared to get to us."

Robin Williams

His is a laugh to behold: a honk, a burst, a blare. Few know his laugh. He does not laugh onstage. Only rarely does it escape in other media. So it startles. You jump a little when you hear it. As though a window had slammed shut. Or a barbell had dropped on cement and bounced. Like an explosion in the bowels of the building. It scares you because you don't expect it; you only expect that he expects it from you.

He is still a kamikaze of the night. In the cockpit of his blue four-wheel-drive vehicle, he purrs through the hushed, sloped arteries of San Francisco, seeking out comedy huts to raid, improv stages to comandeer. He never strikes before midnight, never allows word of his attack to leak out in advance. He likes it that way. It is the only instant gratification he continues to permit himself, the only vice he cannot swear off.

Ever the polite interloper, he will not lunge for the microphone until all of the scheduled comics have finished their sets. As with Berle, legend says he lifts material from others; at worst, he accidentally *absorbs*, but he has honorably paid off those he's wronged. It is one way to apologize for his maelstrom brain. So he lingers outside or on a secluded barstool — usually with a hood yanked down on his forehead — nursing his anonymity before moving in for the kill.

Carrie Fisher and Penny Marshall

One married Simon, one dated Garfunkel. They lived to laugh about this, and them. Fisher and Marshall do not work together (although Carrie once sang "My Guy" on *Laverne and Shirley*); rather, they *emerged* together, as Actresses-Turned-Comic-Forces (Be With You). Theirs is a comic friendship, borne of serendipity and bad hair. They stand in solidarity, like wit and wisdom. Fisher — she of the verbal acuity, the swell riposte, the famous parents — is the writer; Marshall — she of the physical statement, the mumbled aside, the swollen feet — is the director. They defy Hollywood doubters, in whose number they sometimes count themselves. Quoth Carrie, "If wishes were horses, mine would be glue." Still, they are sitting pretty, sitting on top of the world. "No," says Penny, "we're just sitting on top of the bed."

Sid Caesar

Here is mighty Caesar, strong man of comedy. Here is a man who could bench press Mel Brooks, who once dangled Mel Brooks outside a window on the eighteenth floor of Chicago's Palmer House. Here is a man who removed cab doors to make a point and ripped sinks out of walls to demonstrate displeasure. He was not always reasonable, but he was always great. "Everything was done live, you understand?" he will say of his television work, as if to explain why he is peerless. For seven years, he was live, which was herculean, given that he was never not funny. "The first time I saw Caesar it was like seeing a new country," said Neil Simon, who wrote for him. (*Everyone* wrote for Caesar.)   It was a comic empire unlike any other. Caesar once tried to dissect his magic: "There's a fine line between laughter and tears," he said. "When you laugh too hard, you start to cry. When you cry too hard, you start to laugh. When someone doesn't know whether to laugh or cry, your comedy is working."

"Sid was a terrific person. When did he die, by the way?"

MEL BROOKS

Martin Short

"He treats any party as though it were his own birthday party." So say his friends and he cannot deny it. Those who are professionally funny tend toward private despair. Not this fellow. Here is a *celebrant*. "Isn't this the most wonderful time you could possibly have in your life?" he will announce frequently. He can't help it. It is what he does. His characters do the same. Always brimming with hope, they whirl about, mad with euphoria, as though it were Christmas every day. "My heart beats like a jungle drum, I must say," Ed Grimley will say, for of course he must. Which is why nobody will ever believe him when he says, "I'm as doomed as doomed can be, you know."

Dudley Moore

Before a comedian departs the mortal plane, he gives great thought to his exit line, his epitaph. W.C. Fields wanted his headstone to read: I Would Rather Be Here Than in Philadelphia. This fellow wishes for his to read: He Died and Rose Again from the Dead. That is, he does not care to leave laughing as much as return laughing, for which one can hardly blame him. As for his laugh: It is the rare man whose laugh brings laughter to others. His is just such a laugh, a miracle of the upper range, which infects like a benign virus, and makes every witness its victim. "I try to seduce," he has said, of the phenomenon that is him. "I want to attract people. I want their warmth. I want their love."

R. Crumb

Notes from the Underground: Crumb used to dream of becoming a sophisticate, an urban guy, a big commercial artist. He imagined he would drop his unfortunate last name, use his middle name, call himself "Bob Dennis." But then he snapped out of it and took more drugs. He thus begat *Head Comix* and *Zap Comix* and other forms of illustrative insurrection. To some, he is the greatest comic book artist ever, a counterculture Old Master who preferred pulp. He is the cartoon Dylan, inscrutable and prolific. "Who is this Crumb?" Crumb once asked in a strip called "The Many Faces of R. Crumb." Among the postulations he offered: "The enigmatic man of mystery." "The long-suffering, patient artist-saint." "The misanthropic reclusive crank." "The out-of-it dull-witted fool." He concluded: "It all depends on the mood I'm in! Bye all!"

Teri Garr

Her secret marriage to Letterman lasted several months, and in that time the couple lived separately but agreed to take each other's calls, if the opportunity arose. It ended not long after he made her take the shower in his office during a broadcast. (She walked home that night with wet underpants, since she wears underpants whenever her showers are televised.) But he never made a secret of how she made him feel: young, alive, giddy, eager to see her take showers. She, of course, played him like a Stradivarius, feigning the insecurity, the confusion, the dander. So fragile, yet so determined. How he fell for her! And those gams couldn't have made it any easier! It figures that, as a girl, she danced in nine Elvis Presley movies. "Nice guy," she would say of the King, playing coy, as is her wont, driving weak men to distraction, giving others the will to live. Alas, poor Letterman!

Pee-wee Herman

Hours before Pee-wee Herman (P.H.) would sit down with Letterman, Paul Reubens, née Rubenfeld (P.R.), made the S'mores. Working alone backstage in the Green Room, P.R. toiled grimly, diligently. A cigarette hung from his lips. He squinted through the smoke and tore open the pack of graham crackers. He applied the marshmallows, then the Hershey Bar pieces. His manner was precise, uncompromised. But when you tread a fine line, as does P.R. with P.H., perfectionism cannot be undervalued. Once finished, he assembled his bounty on a tray, which he, as P.H., would present to his host, discomfiting him as millions watched. *"I know you are but what am I?"* He bumped past someone who'd been observing his craftsmanship. "Excuse me," said P.R., his voice low, polite, mildly adenoidal. He gave a shy smile, which belonged to P.H., if but for lack of lipstick that he then hurried off to apply.

"The problem, to me," he has said, trying and failing to dismiss his dichotomous being, "is that I have two names, and beyond that, there's not much of a story."

"The first time my mother saw Paul on late-night TV, she called me . . . and she said, 'I don't care what you say, Judy. I am going to buy that boy a suit that fits him. I don't want to see him on television again in a suit that doesn't fit him.'"

JUDY RUBENFELD, PAUL'S MOTHER

Rick Moranis

A nebbish is a nice, but meek fellow at whose expense mirth is made. He is the little man wearing glasses who announces that he ought not to be clobbered because he is a little man wearing glasses. Often, however, he rises up in protest when he can endure no further indignation. At such times, he is more heroic than the greatest of heroes, for he is all of us and we are there with him laying claim to his victory as our own. In comedy, he gets the girl. In life, he has cats.

"Beauty, eh?"

BOB McKENZIE

Johnny Carson and David Letterman

Omnipotence in a time capsule: There will be remembered an epoch in history — the latter portion of the twentieth century, in general — when Comedy itself belonged to the whim of these two men. If you wanted to make a living being funny, they owned your fate, in different ways. How was the one on the left distinct from the one on the right? Here are the basic truths comedians needed to grasp, in order to flourish in that green and desperate period:

Carson was deity. His power was ethereal, his minions vast. When his thumb met forefinger after your Burbank berth, you were annointed. Should he have mouthed the words *funny stuff*, you could go buy a car. His approval was America's approval. Your sitcom deal loomed. The next time you visited, you would probably have been allowed to sit next to his desk and bask in his mythic aura. You would perspire mightily. But rest assured: He would be the friendliest straight man you'd ever meet.

Letterman was mogul. He was comedy's CEO, with cigar (for a while) and furrowed brow. You were always invited to sit down after your stand-up set, but he sat higher than you and tended toward intimidation. You expected thrust and parry. He leaned forward, challenged, and forced you to be funnier or die. If you made him uncomfortable, however, you would not return soon. Try as you could, without his endorsement, you might have survived, but you would never be Hip.

"While I can give Dave zingers once in a while, I could never be on *The Tonight Show* and go, 'Hey Johnny, nice tie!' With Carson, you're in awe."

JAY LENO, BEFORE JOB ADVANCEMENT

Richard Pryor and Gene Wilder

Pain binds men, as does laughter. It is interesting that, of all the people these two could have found for comic allies, they found each other, again and again. Tragedy has visited them both, with all of its requisite terror. But demons beset all comedians in order to make them comedians. Pryor's demons have no precedent, nor does he. There is no encapsulating his significance; he is the one who inspired everyone who arrived after him. He is crazy in a way other men envy — mistakenly so, he might feel. Both he and Wilder excel at high-decibel intensity, where with eyes bulging, they give unique lung power to their joy, outrage and fears. Somehow, they *become* the moment — most notably the moment of panic. "There's a sense of excitement and danger in each scene we play," Wilder said once, "because we really never know what will happen next." Their fine fit made them the first great interracial partnership in comedy, although together they have never seemed merely black and white. They seemed like friends.

Whoopi Goldberg

"A black woman with a Jewish name," said Milton Berle, trying to solve the puzzle. "She doesn't do windows, because she's got a headache."

The Impossible Truth: Child of the projects, welfare mother, Broadway curiosity, dreadlock enthusiast, star — she was born Caryn Johnson, thereby eliciting little notoriety. While working as an actress in a San Diego production of *A Christmas Carol*, she sat backstage one night talking with cast mates about names they would never give their children. "If I was your mother," an observant woman said to Caryn Johnson, "I would have called you Whoopee, because when you're unhappy you make a sound like a whoopee cushion. It sounds like a fart." Since she was open to just this sort of suggestion, she soon became known as Whoopi Cushion. Eventually, her mother intervened. "You won't be taken seriously if you call yourself Whoopi Cushion," she said, sagely, whereupon she offered her daughter the final, indelible solution.

"She suggested Goldberg," recalled Goldberg, swearing that it was so. "She just thought it flowed better. Mothers, you know, they sit and think about shit like this."

Garrison Keillor

Bard of the Lake has nostrils that whistle. They do! Like a zephyr across the prairie! Listen to him there on his broadcasts, giving the News of his hometown, where every week is a quiet week, forcing him to make stuff up as he goes along, wondrous rhapsodies about nothing much really. As this transpires, a vast hunk of America hushes itself, as though Edgar Bergen were about to come on; we shut our collective eyelids in reverie, much like Keillor does while extemporizing matters Wobegon. (The nose whistling fills his magnificent pauses.) In modesty, he has called himself "America's tallest radio humorist," but he is arguably America's finest humorist, period; his published humor pieces have no contemporary equal. He is a different man on paper, lusty and dark, no Lutheran Shy Person especially. "Humor is a knife," he has written, "and what it cuts off doesn't grow back right away."

Spalding Gray

He does go on about himself, especially in the company of strangers. He sits at a desk on a stage and tells stories of his life, in long, detailed paragraphs that do not end in punch lines. (It is the details that make us laugh, for it is in life's minutiae that we best recognize ourselves.) He is the most dedicated of raconteurs, who prefers to voice his experiences, never honing them first on paper. (He's a pageless writer.) The printed word, Gray felt, would transmit none of his urgency. His scheme: "I'll chronicle my life, but I'll do it orally," he told himself, "because to write it down would be in bad faith, it would mean I believed in a future. Each night (onstage) my personal history would disappear on a breath."

It is like therapy, only with more people in the room.

Don Rickles

Sinatra walked into the Big Room. "Come right in, Frankie," said Rickles from the stage. "Make yourself at home. Hit somebody."

Run for cover! What Rickles does is dare you not to kill him. Then he sweats prodigiously, fearing retribution or silence or both or neither. He *should* sweat; few mortals have managed to tease Sinatra about cement shoes and meat hooks, especially while working on the same bill with him. "You're a lovely woman," he has told a thousand ladies in the second row. "Was anyone else hurt in the accident?" Rickles was the first truly great put-down stand-up: "I never met a man I didn't dislike," he has said, exhibiting the desperate bravado of a runt who had to turn over his lunch money to the bully one time too many. Still, he manages to unify us with intimidation: Jews, Wops, Polacks, Micks, Gooks, Colored People: He kids us because we're all the same, deep down inside: wet.

Jackie Mason

Ed Sullivan would hold up two fingers from where he stood in the wings. The gesture meant, "You have two minutes left. The act onstage took heed and finished accordingly. The studio audience also took heed as well as pleasure in watching Sullivan run his show. Sullivan's fingers ruled. "His fingers became more fascinating to people than my best jokes," said the comic. "So I started to make fun of his fingers." On live television, the comic mimicked the host, who saw nothing amusing in finger humor. Fingers were a sacred thing, after all. Suddenly, there it was! Sullivan, aghast, swore that he saw the bird flipped. (He was, in the end, hallucinating.) The comic, a rabbi's son who knew little street vulgarity, found himself condemned and banished. (Such was the potency of Sullivan's wrath.) He did not understand why. "I didn't know from dirty gestures," he said. No one believed him. His career died. The comic was martyred.

Sullivan finally admitted he was wrong, then *he* died.

The comic returned many years later. He was not bitter. He reasoned, "One should appreciate life so much that one shouldn't have time to be bitter."

Smothers Brothers

Rebels with short haircuts: Here were sibling con artists who looked benign, then slipped America conscience when conscience was a dirty word. "The American Legion likes us and so does the left wing," said Tommy, innocently, just as Vietnam began to reorder our ranks. In the Sixties, Tommy and Dickie only played innocent. Beneath their collegiate turtlenecks there beat protesters' hearts. CBS fired them when it became clear that the boys were rabble in disguise, but by then it was too late. They, as Network Comedians, had actually suggested that the democracy was deeply flawed! (It was a precedent in 1969.)

They were acid vaudeville: brothers who argue, dumb one on guitar, smart one on bass. They sang folk songs, replacing the middle verses with Tom's foolery: "Come on, Mike! Pull on those oars, baby!" (This from "Michael, Row the Boat Ashore.") In the real world, Tommy (the elder) ran things — dumb as a fox, he was the brains, he fought the fights, he got the girls; Dickie (the younger) was silent partner who went home to the family at night. ("The comic is driven, involved in detail, the timing, the creation of the act," said Tommy, explaining their chemistry. "The straight man enjoys life.") Tommy once turned to Bette Davis during an appearance on *The Tonight Show* and asked, with his crooked grin, "Hey, do you want to mess around?" (She guffawed.) He could do whatever he wanted, but what he wanted most was a platform.

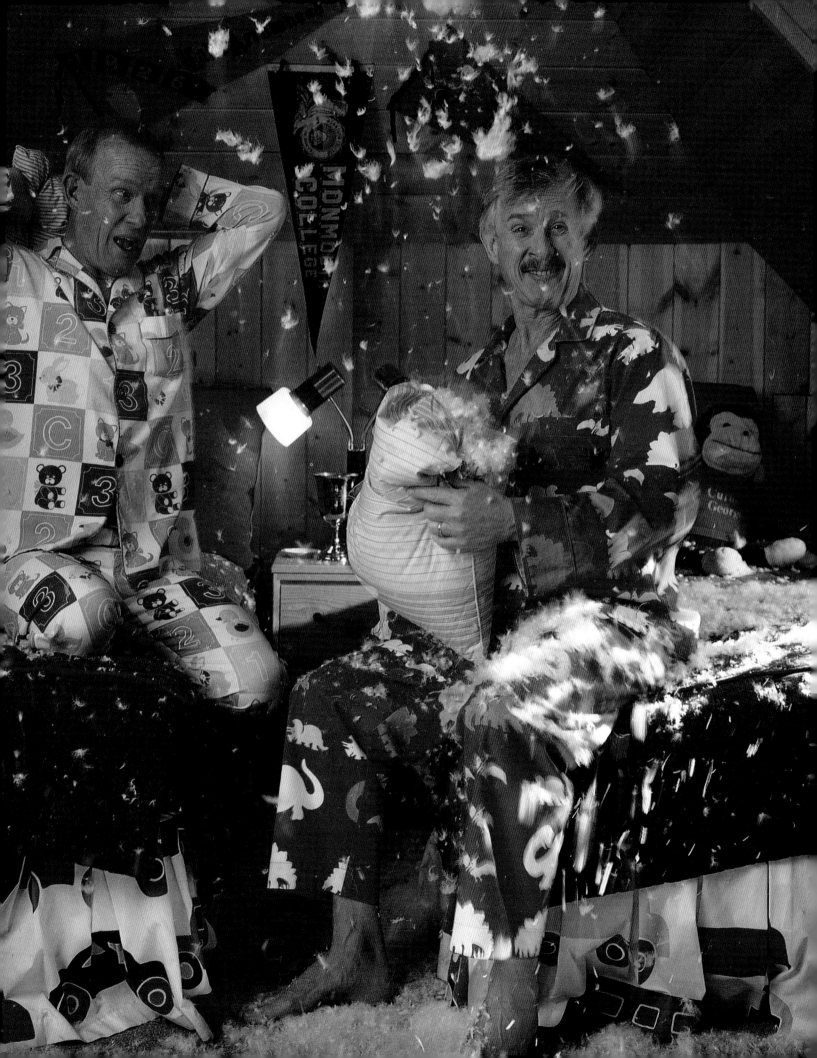

Eddie Murphy

His friends call him Money. He looks like money. He looks crisp, controlled. He stares straight ahead and seems to notice no one, but sees all and hears even more. Unless he's erupting into his deft repertoire of character voices, his presence is shy, inscrutable. Usually, he is sullen, almost somber — but this creates a quiet aura of power. You feel him before you see him; first you see his men. He is insulated by bodies, a cleaving pack of old friends and relations on the payroll. These are Eddie's Boys; they attend to him, fortify him, laugh at him approvingly.

But make no mistake: It is Eddie who Takes Care of Business. In this way, Eddie is like Elvis. In many ways, he is like Elvis. He *likes* Elvis. His office is stocked with arcane Presleyana of all sorts. "Elvis looked like every hair was where it was supposed to be," explains Eddie, who is known throughout his household for interminable rituals spent before mirrors, combing and recombing his hair. Often when he can think of nothing to say, he elects to become Elvis. "Heybabybossanovababy," he croons, in Elvis Presley's voice. "Thankyouthankyouverrrrmuch." Fifty million fans can't be wrong.

"Let me rub your head for luck, boy!"

> Col. Tom Parker, to Eddie Murphy,
> at the crap table of the Las Vegas Hilton

Jonathan Winters

Life is his toy. He carries it with him wherever he goes. He is the supreme Only Child, forever left to his own devices. He must amuse himself, and does, which amuses others, for which he could not be happier. He is the opposite of self-conscious. He wears costumes around the house and the neighborhood and beyond, because it pleases him to do so. "You're asking for it!" his wife warns him. *Exactly*, he thinks. Every time he puts on a new hat, he is someone else, someone astonishing. His daughter wrote a poem for him, in which she said, "You taught me to be proud to be strange."

"I've worked hard on keeping the child in me alive," he has said. "I always find that it's the wrong people who ask, 'Aren't you ever going to grow up?'"

"Jonathan has taught me that the world is open for play, that anything and everybody is mockable, in a wonderful way."

ROBIN WILLIAMS

Jon Lovitz

"Get to know me!" he begged, and so we would try, but he is a man who surrounds himself always with beautiful women, and it is difficult to get a sense of him alone, unfettered from the sycophants who prey on his every free moment. He is said to be a pensive man, and perhaps that is why women are drawn to him. Also, he has a lovely singing voice, almost operatic in nature, and he enjoys nothing more than sharing it with whomever he encounters. So enamored is he of his vocal skill that he has been known to take a megaphone and croon into the vast and verdant hillsides, "Helloooooooooooo, Hollywooooood!" Other times he will simply sing in the bathroom. Ah, the acoustics! How the women grow faint!

Sam Kinison

Men had grown soft and needed an example. After Kinison emerged from the depths of the pond, much would be made of The Wild Man, the warrior in all of us, extinct for generations. Men would go on ceremonial retreats and howl in the woods, trying to find their lost maleness. Kinison had been screaming for a while, by then. He had ranted at the heavens, as only a former evangelist could (the license plates on his Corvette read EXREV), loosing a sonic boom of dyspeptic outrage. (Once, long ago on his pulpit, he fired a .38 at the church ceiling, so as to urge his flock to fill the collection plates.) His bile is so undiluted, it is funny. As he would put it, "Oh! OH! AAAAUGH!" And ears would bleed. "I think people get anger out of their system by seeing me," he has explained. "You can't ignore anger."

Billy Crystal and Alan King

"Comedy without pathos is like sitting down to a meal without bread," Gleason said. "Funny had better be sad somewhere," said Jerry Lewis. "It is better to look good than to feel good," said Crystal, whose work makes us feel bittersweet when it is working best. "Oooooh, I hate when that happens," he will say, empathizing always, a sad, smiling medium for disembodied pain and reckoning. His face was made for pathos. It is the face of a thousand men, all men who feel much. "To me," he has said, "a stand-up is a man or a woman who goes out in front of people emotionally naked and talks about real things."

"I deal in truth," said King, who embodies the real thing. "When I talk about my wife, every guy has to recognize *his* wife." King was the big angry man with the cigar, who bled onstage, elegantly so, and wore expensive suits. ("He is the only comedian I know who spends money like a drunken admiral," Jack Benny once observed.) "Alan is the Museum of Comedy," said Crystal, one of King's most loyal subjects, who culls his trade secrets. For instance, on how to dress for comedy: "He said to put my shoes on before my pants," Crystal revealed, completely serious. "That way you don't break your crease." Because it is better to look good.

Robert Townsend

He wishes to be Cosby. As a mimic, he does a fine Cosby, a Cosby equalled only perhaps by his friend Eddie Murphy, who is, of course, the antithesis of Cosby. (Eddie wished to be Pryor.) Townsend directed Murphy in *Raw,* a profane concert film of the sort Cosby loathes. He directed himself doing Murphy in his first film, *Hollywood Shuffle,* a comic exposé of the plight of the contemporary black actor — a plight that included a wry cattle call for "an Eddie Murphy type." (His outrage is absurdist, not militant, yet its sting is much the same.) He wrote that film with brother-in-sly-revolt Keenen Ivory Wayans. (These two form the nucleus of the comic encampment Murphy calls the Black Pack.) Of them all, Townsend is most gentle, "a man of irrefutable sweetness," as one critic put it. He and Wayans once drove across America together with hopes of writing another movie. "Four hours into the ride and it was, 'Don't say shit to me!'" he recalls. "We argued and stuff and then we wrote the script. It's the yin-and-yang thang. Keenen is the bad boy and I'm the semi-good boy."

Eric Idle

George Harrison, who is wise in such matters, believed that the karmic soul of the Beatles was spiritually bequeathed directly to the Monty Python fellows. If so, and even if not, Idle got to be the Cute One. Know what we mean? Nudge, nudge. Usually, he wrote alone, a Python island unto himself, but was no less depraved than his mates. After the release of their *Holy Grail*, he was asked what the group planned next. "I said, rather flippantly, 'Jesus Christ's lust for glory,'" he recalled later. From this — a fine offensive lie, borne of exasperation — there sprang *The Life of Brian*, which according to that most contentious of Pythons, John Cleese, was "our masterpiece." We'll say no more! Nudge, nudge.

Sandra Bernhard

She's not so scary.

Up close, that perilous face with its incendiary features melts easily into lovely repose. Up close, her preternatural aggressiveness seems to be nothing more than sheer girlish enthusiasm. She emphatically grabs other people's arms, wrists, thighs, but her touch is conspiratorial, not obtrusive. She is fond of telling people she loves them. She is not insincere — just effusive.

Example: One hot evening, she impulsively clamps a headlock on a large, unsuspecting pit bull. A *stranger's* pit bull, no less, on a gritty street corner in downtown New York. She spied her quarry hunkered on the sidewalk, slurping a piña colada out of a paper cup. Now she has it pinned to the pavement. "This dog is *so fuckin' cute!*" she squeals, vigorously nuzzling the pooch as it drinks. "Hiiiiiiiii, sweetie piiiiiie. Little bubba! Little booger! Little *boooooooger!*"

If the dog is afraid of being bitten, it gives no sign.

"Before she came around, I was somebody in this town. Now all people do is call me for quotes on Sandra."

MADONNA LOUISE CICCONE

Soupy Sales

"Listen," he once told director Jonathan Miller, "the guy who's doing the bit is the *first* to know it isn't working." Dr. Miller had been trying to teach stagecraft to the former Milton Supman, who was preparing for his Broadway comedy debut. "You mustn't discharge the energy, Soup," instructed the great British director. "You must hold the tension like a coiled watch spring." This was an unnatural act for Soupy, but he obeyed. Later, he wept when he read the reviews.

He was a big noisy adult who acted like an idiot on a children's television show, for which he was beloved. Idiot energy is a thrill to behold; it can never be made elegant. His commerce was the seltzer spritz, the pratfall, the unspeakable pun, and the pie-in-the-face. He met his first pie in 1950; he lowball-guesses that 20,000 pies have flown since. Fortunately, his is a face that improves with topping. "The pies are filled with shaving cream," he confessed, revealing trade tricks. "We *used* to use egg whites, but they spoil, and whipped cream is too hard to clean off."

Dana Carvey and Victoria Jackson

He becomes the characters; she is the character. She is a human bubble, fun to watch float in and out of view. For her, that is enough. He is deceiving, a malleable young man who is everyone and no one. There are times, it is said, when he does not recognize himself in the mirror. He is Bush, for instance, because we need someone to be Bush. "Wouldn't be prudent," he will say, making one, who may be unlikable to some, likable to all. As Enid Strict, church lady, he is she, adamantly so: "She's not a man in a dress," Carvey has gently asserted, in the third person. "She's a real lady." (He blurs, therefore he is.) *Saturday Night Live* godfather Lorne Michaels has said of Carvey, "He is one of those rare comedians who leaves no fingerprints." And, of course, that is special.

Michael Keaton

The eyes have it. Comedy is perspective, slightly askew. It is about how we see things. When a man has crazy eyes, as has Keaton, he sees life especially differently. His wily eyeworks flare and careen beneath great arched brows, which portend grand business, anyway. (In big-screen close-ups, it is said that a Keaton brow, aloft, stands the height of an average door; only Nicholson, in this regard, is his peer.) We see the movable parts of his brain through his eyes: the pistons firing, the hammers pounding, the squirrels on treadmills. What he sees: Watching old movies, for instance, he sees hats. As in, "Get your hat! We're going downtown." *But I don't have a hat.* "Whaddya mean ya don't have a hat!" *I don't have one.* "Well, can you borrow a hat?"

He gives a demonstration: At a Lakers game, one spring night, his eyes interpret all humanity that courses through the Great Western Forum. Spotting a man with an unusually large forehead, he says, "Runs a windshield-endurance school." Then a bald man wearing a vile-colored blazer: "I hate to say it, but that coat's *phlegm brown.* The guy must own a Lincoln dealership." And three tall, thin, solemn men in suits: "These guys look like they should come to your house with books."

The eyes have it, somewhere.

Jerry Lewis

He understood his importance long before the French did. He is Father of Havoc, great foe of Decorum. He defies inattention. Look at him or he will perish. *"Notice me,"* he has said. "As the writer of Jerry Lewis, I can tell you that the premise of the character has always been that simple and basic." He loves to speak of Jerry Lewis, as though Jerry Lewis was someone he wasn't, which must at times be a consoling notion. (He was born Joseph Levitch and five years later entered Show Business, which has ever since been his life.) Look at him look at Jerry Lewis: "I'm watching Jerry Lewis like I'm watching Jerry Lewis in anything I do — very objectively, because either he's good or he's bad." When he is both, he is best, in a way. The greatest clowns are not as artful as they are energetic. And no man has ever known adrenaline like this man has.

"He's just a complicated guy. His personality can be hard to take. But when he became a star, it wasn't because people were interested in his personality. People weren't necessarily interested in the real Charlie Chaplin, either."

MARTIN SHORT

"Lewis is one of the most gifted and natural comic talents we've ever had. I've laughed hysterically at many of his films. I've seen him live and loved him."

WOODY ALLEN

John Belushi

"I hate the fucking Bees!" he would bellow, referring to the Killer Bees sketches that so demeaned him. "I want to burn those fucking Bee costumes!" Now, when Studio 8-H falls still, they can sometimes hear the voice boom, loud protestations that haunt the rafters. His brother in blues, Aykroyd the Ghostbuster, swears that, whenever he visits, he can see Belushi Ectoplasm stalking the NBC corridors. O sweet querulous ghost! Were he still alive and bouldering about, wouldn't he be a wistful Belushi? A Belushi who occasionally fingered the grip of his samurai blade and hiked one of those magnificent Belushi eyebrows, contemplating one last charge? But *noooooooooo*.

"He was like the world's largest puppy. . . . He once wanted to take me to Disneyland and I said, 'Forget it, John. Going there with you would be like going there with another Matterhorn!' John was his own Disneyland, with better rides."

CARRIE FISHER

Howie Mandel

Why Be a Comic? To earn Mother's Approval, of course. To earn her devotion, her attention, her heart. To be able to say, "Mom, I'm playing in a little place out on Sepulveda Boulevard tonight," and then see her sitting right there, just like she promised, fresh from the beauty parlor, wearing her best fur and her best red dress, laughing and cheering and loving you like she has never loved you before. It is as simple as that.

Catherine O'Hara

Characters swallow her, leaving behind no traces of whom she ever was. "When I pretend to be someone else, I go to the depths of nothingness," she has said. We remember the minx Lola Heatherton, who wished to bear our babies, her lip quivering into a saucy pout. But the woman behind Lola? "My personality doesn't shine through," she has said, "and that makes *me* hard to remember. People always say,'You and all those other girls were so great on *SCTV.*' When I say it was just two of us, they look baffled."

Jerry Seinfeld

His only hook is that he is the hookless comedian. He could've been the Big Pants comic, but the premise seems difficult to sustain. So he makes do being remarkably unremarkable, a Zen Buddhist fancier whose work is spare and impeccable — much like his apartment. His great friend Leno has long likened the Seinfeld digs to "a hospital room with a stereo." Privately, he is the young wise man of comedy, who dispenses profound truth to his hungry brethren. For instance: "There is no such thing as a Comedy Star," he has put forth. "Once you think you're a star, you're no comedian. A comedian is someone like Us. A star is somebody like Cary Grant or DeNiro. We don't know who they are, we don't *want* to know. But a comedian has got to be somebody I *do* know and can relate to. So a comedy star, to me, is a contradiction in terms."

Emo Phillips

He is considered by many. Sometimes, if you stare long enough, you can almost see his brain bleed. A fashion plate, he used to buy Nehru jackets like they were going out of style. He became a comedian to get people to stop laughing at him. He understands coleslaw the way other men understand carburetors. When he was ten, his parents moved to Downers Grove, Illinois. When he was twelve, he found them. He is, he likes to say, "quite handy with the ladies." Do not dismiss him. Says Emo, "You've got to get up pretty early in the morning to catch me peeking through your bedroom window."

Phyllis Diller

If this was your mother and she behaved like this in front of your friends, you would wish to die. Thus begat a career. She was our first domestic goddess, and unlike domestic goddesses who have come along since, she dressed the part. Gussied as such, she is at once repulsive and glamorous, like a pink champagne hangover. She brays like a coyote and owns 340 ugly wigs and she won't go away and damned if there isn't something pleasantly reassuring about that.

Danny DeVito

In comedy, it is good to be small and noisy. Much like a hand grenade, you will draw attention away from matters that may be more apparent, but ultimately less intriguing. As such, you become larger than life itself, and you still have plenty of extra leg room.

Robert Klein

Smart comics revere Klein because Klein is among the smartest of smart comics. (Look! He reads! Even his son reads! These Kleins — what smart guys!) He is the oldest of young comics; the youngest of old comics. He can play any room, for any crowd, and usually he will also sing. ("The thing about Klein," Leno once told a friend, cringing as only Leno can, "is that he *sings*." Leno, by the way, reveres Klein.) He was the first to do the Scary Movie Noise: *Oooo-weee-oooooooooo*. And the Dentist's Drill Noise, too, for which no italics can do justice. Both are noises copied the world over by lesser beings. But Klein is a man of words, not noises. He will make you *believe*, selling setups with unequaled conviction and intelligence. Witness perfection: "I don't want to bore you with lectures, but it turns out that George Washington, for his time and his task, was a great man. He was tall and imposing and brave and the right man at the right time and . . . he would have been hung had we lost the revolution. He is, in truth, the father of our country. And I'm sure he'd be very, very thrilled to know that we sacredly observe his birthday each year with a mattress sale."

Paula Poundstone

On Working With Chimps: To work with a Chimp, you must be stoic. You must be willing to sacrifice dignity in exchange for peals of hearty laughter. (Usually, this is considered a fair trade.) With a banana, you can buy the world. Understand that whatever you say and do will never be as interesting as your partner. Shedding happens. You will acquire new, unfamiliar odors; accept this and you will thrive. Teeth marks often heal, leaving no scar whatsoever. And finally: Monkey lips *feel* like human lips, but taste differently.

Matt Groening

Conceit for profit: He named his firstborn Homer Groening, but then he is himself the son of a Homer. And a Margaret. For sisters, he has a Lisa and a Maggie. There is no real Bart (anagram for *brat*, rhymes with Matt), unless, of course, he gazes deeply, darkly, unforgivingly, into a mirror. "The best part of all this," he said, just as popular culture took his orange-hued, pop-eyed family to its breast, "is seeing Bart Simpson graffiti on freeway underpasses. The worst part is seeing Bart Simpson graffiti on the side of my house — somebody wrote HOME OF BART there. So I guess what I'm saying is, the best part is graffiti on *other people's* property."

Steve Martin

He was the rock king. He wore white. He showed up better in white. He filled stadiums. Comedians don't play stadiums anymore. Come to think of it, they didn't play stadiums then, either. But those were the Banjo Years, and he was quite the picker. (They say he's stopped playing altogether now.) Remember the way he always asked to be excused? Why, people begged him to beg their pardon! They moved their mouths to the routines they loved best. Wild, he said. And crazy, he also said. Then came the dancing! So lively. But so precise. Like Astaire. Only not.

"Carl Reiner used to say, 'You know what your act is? You look like a guy who looked at Fred Astaire and said, Hey, I can do that — watch!' Really described me perfectly."

It was passive aggressive bliss, a rebellion against rebellious comedy, *anti-comedy*, he calls it now. (Lenny Bruce was storm and sweat; Martin was breeze and balloons. Well, *vigorous* breeze and balloon *animals*.) He worked inside of quotation marks. "Pauline Kael said it: I was a guy acting like a comedian and the audience was acting like an audience. It was all like a big show-business joke." He lists his attributes like so: "I was real energetic and real high and real dumb." But he is, of course, being stingy with himself. It was stupid anarchy, yes — but choreographed to the letter. Like Astaire. Only not.

"To spend time with him is like being alone. Except when he is being funny."

TOMMY SMOTHERS

Lily Tomlin

She fills the stage with all of the women she imagines herself to be. It is a crowded expanse. So, too, is her soul. "I'm sharing my life with you tonight," she used to say to her audiences, "and when I go outside, I hope I don't find it in the gutter with a Hush Puppy skid mark on it." Lily's women are bred of humanity and conscience and best belong to the theater, where the lighting is better. Without costume changes or revolving sets, she populates, then colors a universe, by simply (!) physicalizing words. When alone, she practices, mumbling to herself, pacing, emitting odd noises, contorting her long countenance, like any one of a thousand street people in private reverie. She is, then, the First Bag Lady of the Stage. "I do not make up things," she once said, as the immortal imp, Edith Ann. "That is lies. Lies is not true. But the truth could be made up if you know how.

"And that's the truth."

"I love Lily. I have a thing about her, a little crush. She's so good I get embarrassed, I get in awe of her. . . . Something about her is very sensual, isn't it? You know, when she works, I'd like to ball her in all them different characters she does sometimes. Wouldn't you?"

RICHARD PRYOR

Bob Newhart

He reasons with chaos, losing always. He blinks rapidly, as if to fan off incoming crackpots. He prefers not to be touched or to be dressed in foolish costumes. Because of this, we thrill to see him hugged on camera, while wearing a pirate's hat. He is the quietest giant of comedy: Like Benny before him, it is what Newhart doesn't say that is so pungent. "Flies die on his face," his friend Don Rickles has often said. Meaning, the flies die bored.

Yet the Newhart face is not exactly bland. It is the kind of face that looks like a headache, albeit a mild, friendly one. To this end, young men dedicate drinking contests to his face, for collegiate sport. The rules: In reruns, whenever stammering psychologist Bob Hartley is greeted ("Hi, Bob!") — and he is, it seems, greeted with absurd frequency — players must chug gamely. "I hope I've done more in my life than to be remembered by innumerable hangovers on college campuses," laments the Oft-Greeted One. "I like to think it's a testimonial to the quality of the old show. I heard there's one episode with forty-four Hi Bob's in it."

Bob Elliott and Chris Elliott

Now that Bob is Rayless — alas, the untimely death of Ray Goulding ended one of comedy's greatest partnerships — he has been known to work with his son, the fine character actor whose portrayal of The Guy Under the Seats, among other guys, has thrilled millions. What these men share, besides doleful eyes and soaring foreheads, is a rarefied knack for sincere insincerity, a mastery of the Deadpan, if you will. That is, nothing either one of them has ever said is likely to be true. "Bob Elliott's shadow was a long one, indeed," his son once wrote, "and I would soon learn that no matter how hard I tried to walk in his path without actually stepping in his footsteps, I would always be wearing his socks."

"I remember when I learned that Chris was the son of the Great Bob Elliott, I assumed it was simply an ill-considered late-life adoption. I still think that was the case, perhaps even linked to some kind of a wager gone sour."

DAVID LETTERMAN

Mike Meyers

"There are comedians in this business that are perched on the edge of danger," said Dan Aykroyd, discoursing on qualities he admires in others. "You're not sure what's going to come next." Myers, pictured here leaping from a Manhattan rooftop where certain death waits below, may be just such a comedian. He is the classic comic ingenue who, as a boy, dreamt of becoming a big *Saturday Night Live* star, then one day awoke to discover that he was exactly that. "No way!" he would say, as the excellent Wayne Campbell, of *Wayne's World*. ("*Way!*" we would have to parry.) Onstage, "when we're waving goodnight," he has said, "I'm thinking, God, I can't believe it. Dan Aykroyd used to be here." Dreams are nothing if not dangerous.

Albert Brooks

He is never *on* and he is never *off*. For this reason, he is considered less a comic, more an oracle. His name is spoken reverently by those who know comedy. To them, he is Albert, simply Albert. As if to say, We are here, but he is Over There. As such, he is known as Comedy's Recluse. Imprisoned by impossibly high standards, he has become a show business hermit: He is uncompromised, therefore unseen. Upon completing his films (when he chooses to make them), he is nowhere to be found unless you go over to his house.

Because there is no place else he deigns to put it, he keeps most of his comedy to himself: Above the desk in his office, there hangs a framed letter. Few visitors ever notice it, but that is inconsequential. Crudely typed on smudged New York Yankees stationery, the letter is dated August 5, 1928, and is addressed to a Dr. Herbert Stevens, at Mount Sinai Hospital. It reads as follows:

> *Dear Dr. Stevens:*
>
> *Last Sunday when I visited Tommy on the fourth floor, I promised him I would hit a home run. As you may have heard, I ground out four times that day. I understand that little Tommy has since passed on. In the future, I won't promise anything specific to the children. I'll just do what I can.*
>
> *My best,*
> *Babe*

Albert's secretary typed the letter exactly as he had dictated it to her. The smudges were her idea.

126

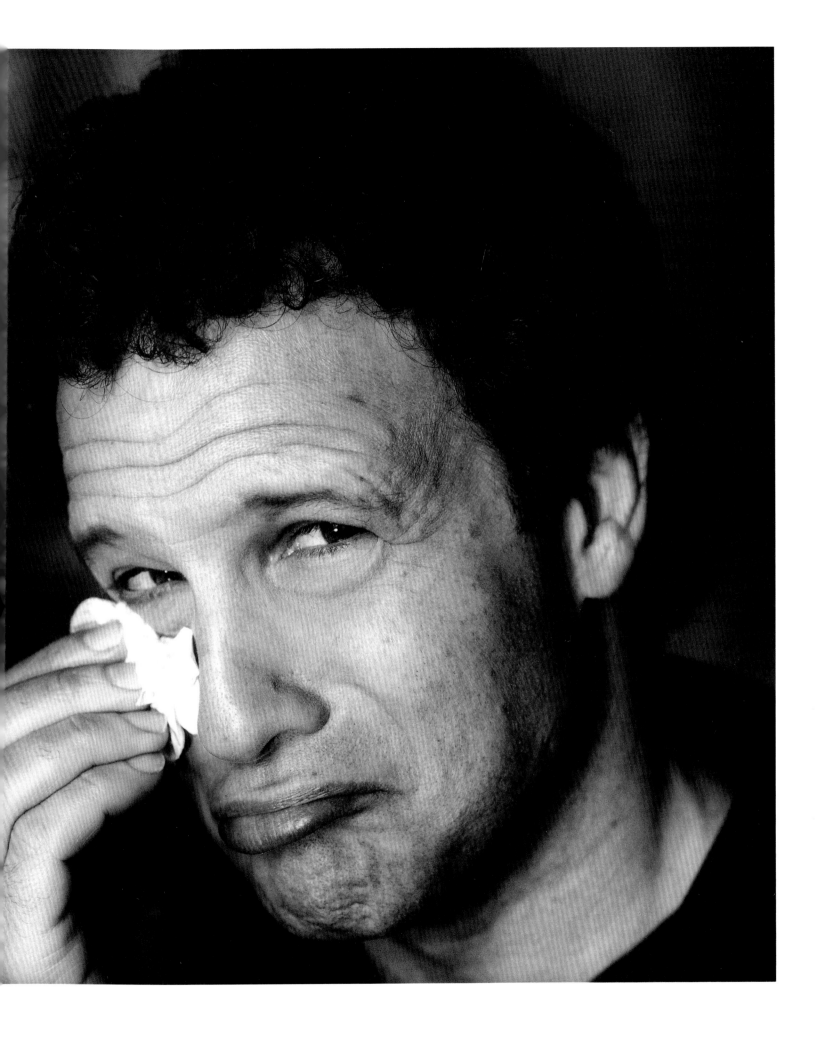

Richard Lewis

With apologies to Edvard Munch, the subject wishes to call the picture at right *The Scream, Part Two.*

This must be said with all due respect: He is worse than he seems. What is glorious about Lewis is that reality exceeds the act. Offstage, he *could* be a man who wears pastels, who throws back his head to laugh, who struts jauntily and arranges Sunday tennis matches. He could host lavish dinner parties for large groups of people, many of whom he may not even know, then sing around the piano. He could own handsome dogs and frolic with them on manicured lawns.

And yet, this will never be so. Lewis dwells in blackness. He sips his mimosas in the lounge of the St. James Club on Sunset and he writes on yellow pads about what is horrible. "Mind if I write while you talk?" he says to a friend, who is sharing relationship nightmares with him. The friend bares his soul; Lewis writes. *Is he taking notes? Is he working on his own material? Is he even listening?* Lewis writes everywhere, on any available surface; always his hands are blotched with black ink. His underwear has even been blackened on occasion, although this puzzles Lewis as much as anyone. Do not judge him. Do not mock his posture: Gravity pulls on him more unforgivingly than it does us. Quite frankly, at least he has his health.

Mary Tyler Moore

She is, of course, the cat's meow. Owning a smile that turns on the world is a responsibility not to be taken lightly, and she has always been more than accommodating when it came to displaying it. As such, many nothing days were suddenly all made worthwhile. It was on Mary's desk that the Kleenex was kept, and so the group of them, bunched together in sweet regret, shuffled *en masse* across the Minneapolis newsroom to dry their eyes and find composure. "What is a family?" she said to her co-workers. "They're just people who make you feel less alone and really loved." Off, then, they marched to Tipperary, and, the last one to go, she doused the lights behind them.

"She's shit free."

Gloria Steinem

130

Steven Wright

"I was once walking through the forest alone," he says, "and a tree fell right in front of me, and I didn't hear it." Sad, monotonous, surreal fellow here has a large seashell collection that he keeps scattered on beaches all over the world. "Maybe you've seen it." Of course, his is a small world, but he wouldn't want to paint it. Nevertheless, he is comedy's Dali, whose strokes are quick, askew, fine. He uses no segues. He speaks in forked haiku. He asks women, "Do you live around here often?" He doesn't write his jokes. "Someone in my head tells them to me." The reason he talks the way he talks is that when he first performed, he froze. It was mistaken for attitude. He stayed frozen. He — and no one else — might ask, "Is this a decaffeinated coffee table book?"

Milton Berle

Sometimes a cigar is just a cigar. Here, of course, it is something else: a tradesman's torch, an implement of punctuation, a smoke signal. Once, when a man wished to be funny, he needed a cigar. If the same man wished to be *extremely* funny, he needed a *dress* and a cigar.

"What the hell is Lucille Ball?" this particular man once said to Lucille Ball. *"Me, in drag."* The Thief of Bad Gags, who has seen everything and borrowed much of what he saw, peers through a gray cloud at a world that always threatens to disappoint him. Beneath the bluster, he is a large meticulous man, the legendary joke archivist whose files burst with several lifetimes of material, some of it actually his own. Some nights, he sits in smoke at the back of Nate 'n' Al's delicatessen in Beverly Hills, reading Lotto tickets with cronies who need the luck more than he does. He needs something else. "Go ahead and laugh," he would say, defiantly. "Please."

ACKNOWLEDGMENTS

The photographer, the writer, the editor, the designer and the producer
of this book wish to acknowledge and thank the following people whose generous help
and cooperation were essential to its creation:

Mark Rutenberg, Margaret Kimura, Cynthia K. Cruz, Kimmie Messina, Jetty Stutzman,
Annette Zeglen, Laurie Matsushima, Allison Sherwood, Raymond Lee, Jonathan Skow,
Iris Lewis, Irene Albright, Charnelle Rhodes, Christine and Steven Eason, Tony Di Zinno,
Julian Kaiser, Kip Corley, Steve Crise, Rick Elden, Alice Arnold, Liz Gadbois,
William Knight, Georgia Hodges, Daniel Roebuck, Ellen Roebuck, Phillip Nardulli,
Riki Arnold, Nick's Color Lab, Arnold Lipsman, Buddy Morra, Marcia Williams,
Jackie Besher, Terrie Williams, Tracy Schiffman, Don and Shana Passman,
Todd Schiffman, Joye Barth, David and Annie T. Auchincloss, Leigh Bradford,
Lisa Steinmeyer, Elizabeth A. Williams, Denise Sfraga, Jennifer Hirshlag, Charles Jarman,
Tracy Barone, David Handelman, Genelle Izumi-Uyekawa, Richard Lalich,
David Rensin, Jeffrey Ressner, John Rezek, Bob Wallace, Bob Love, Mary Astadourian,
Lacey Ashley, Dale Hoffer, Holly George-Warren, Dana Goodall DeAngelis,
Christina Eckerson, Lindley Boegehold, and especially Laura Nolan.

Bonnie Schiffman also thanks Harold Sweet for all his hard work and Robert Trachtenberg
for being such a pal. Thanks, too, to Earl Klasky for the idea, Bill Bartman for his generosity
and Jann S. Wenner for his support.

And, finally, thanks to the comedians — for everything.

SARAH LAZIN BOOKS

PHOTO EDITOR: LAURIE KRATOCHVIL
DESIGNER: NANCY BUTKUS

THE TEXT IS SET IN MONOTYPE ITALIAN OLD STYLE, WITH DISPLAY IN ONYX.

PRINTED BY PRINCETON POLYCHROME PRESS
BOUND BY ACME BOOKBINDING COMPANY, INC.